Understanding Digital Photography | The Only Beginners Guide You'll Ever Need

Master photography in 6 steps with practical tips and hands-on examples

Fabrizio Miccichè

Copyright © 2019 Fabrizio Miccichè

All rights reserved.

ISBN 13: 978-1-7094-3105-0

Table of Contents

The Art of Photography 1

Chapter 1: setting the basics 4

    The Genres of Photography 5

    The Skills to Capture 7

    Perfect Imperfect 7

    Rule of Thirds 8

    Anatomy of DSLR 10

    Viewfinder 12

    Holding your camera 12

    JPEG vs. RAW 15

    Light in photography 16

    Explaining Color Temperature 16

    White Balance 17

    Camera Lenses Explained 17

    Introducing Lenses 17

    How to Choose Your First Lens 19

Chapter 2: Understanding Aperture 22

    What is f-stop? 24

    Shooting in Aperture Priority Mode 25

    Exercise 1: Keeping Everything in Focus 26

    Exercise 2: Using Shallow Depth of Field for Portraits 27

Chapter 3: Learning and understanding Shutter Speed 28

- Exercise 3: Free motion with the fast shutter speed 31
- Exercise 4: Silky water with slow shutter speed 33
- Exercise 5: Panning for Sharpness and Blur 34

Chapter 4: Introducing ISO 36
- When to Use Low or High ISO 37
- Take control of the ISO and avoid the auto ISO mode 37
- ISO for Landscapes, Architectural and Studio Photography 38
- Adjusting High ISO to Capture Landscape at Night 38
- ISO for Architectural Photography 39
- ISO for Studio Photography 39

Chapter 5: Exposure 40
- Explaining Histograms 41

Chapter 5: What is Focus? 44
- Continuous vs Single-Servo Autofocus 45
- Autofocus Area Modes 45
- Where to Focus 47
- Where to focus in landscape photography? 48
- Recompose your shot 50

Chapter 6: From automatic to manual mode 51
- Tips to get the best shots 51

Concluding Thoughts 56

" You don't take a photograph, you make it."

by Ansel Adams

The Art of Photography

P hotography is a unique technique that allows us to capture light with a camera to create an image. Depending on the equipment it is used, one might able to capture a colorful forest path, a stunning portrait or visualize the milky way on a beautiful night at the mountains typically invisible to the human eye.

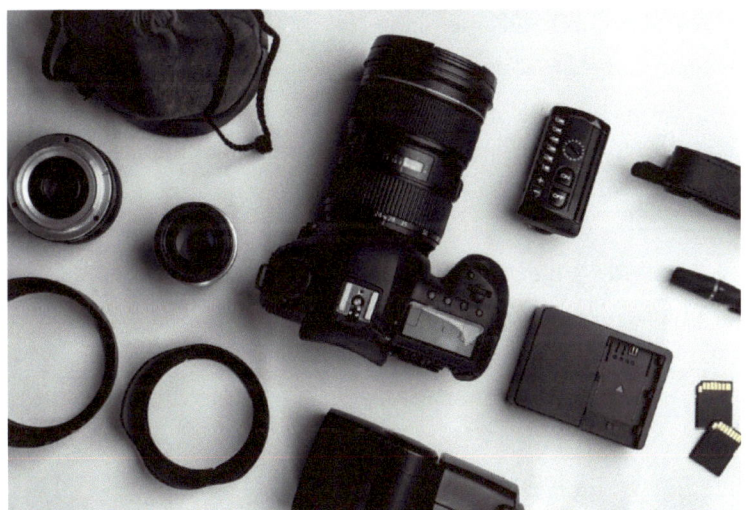

There is a big misconception that good photography comes with expensive gears. How *many cameras* do you actually need? This narrows down to what works for you, what you can afford, and what type of photography you are after. Just keep in mind that the best camera system is whatever one you feel the most comfortable using and working with. Virtually every major camera manufacturer produces high-quality equipment capable of capturing stunning images. Remember that a camera is just a tool, and the photographer is the one who takes the shot. It is the photographer who evaluates the scene, decides how to expose, frames the scene and ultimately snaps the shutter button. There is a lot more that goes into photography than the camera.

Nowadays, many people, sadly, opt for mobile phone photography because they are easy to use, useful to store, and share beautiful memories at the easy of your fingertips. However, it is important to understand that comparing a smartphone to a DSRL is the same as comparing apples to oranges. Amongst the various differences between DSLR cameras and smartphones, the sensor size is one to highlight. The sensor is the core technology of how a camera works. Its function is to capture all the light coming in through the lens and the larger the size of the sensor, the more light it can capture. This means that the more light a sensor can capture, the more detailed and true your photos look. And that alone is enough to clarify why a DSRL remains a valuable tool towards good and true photography.

Often, I hear debates about megapixels: please stop counting megapixels! Megapixels are one of the most common ways of advertising the quality of cameras, especially relatively low-end cameras, aimed at the mass market. Instead of worrying about the number of megapixels, focus on specific features such as sensor size and processor of your camera. And most importantly, focus on mastering the photography basics that in turn will enable you to create your dream images.

The art of photography is dedicated to the unique skills of the photographer. It's the skill of the photographer who turns an ordinary object into an unordinary subject.

At first, one might be overwhelmed by the dozens of functionalities that your camera has. However, it is very unlikely that you need them all and the camera remains the photography tool you need to create your image. Will you need to know all the ins and outs of your camera to start taking photos? Surely not! All you need for now is a basic set of knowledge and understanding to get started. The more you familiarize and practice with your camera, the more you will improve and master your skills and technique.

This book is dedicated to everyone who is interested in learning photography in a practical way. The basic tools one needs are explained and enriched with practical examples to set you off for success and start shooting. Remember that after learning the basics, the best way to improve your photography is shooting.

Chapter 1: Setting the Basics

The photograph is something that captures the distinctive perspective of reality, has a deeper hidden meaning, and has a story to tell. A picture is a valuable image, a brilliant idea, and the capability of the subject to keep the attention of the viewer attached to it. A great photo is an image that has a special meaning and conveys emotions to the viewer. After all, it is said that a picture is worth a thousand words. In today's world filled with technology, many claims to be a photographer, but not every picture it is taken is a photograph. The ability to transform a picture into a photo is a skill.

What Makes a Good Photograph? A good photograph is quite a big word in the world of photography and its definition might be different for every person. Frequently, it can be a unique perspective, a usual composition, or a beautiful view captured in a unique way.

From the photojournalism's perspective, a good photograph can be any useful piece of evidence, a rare historical memory or a valuable photograph of famous personality even if it is blurry or little out of focus.

Sometimes it is claimed that a good photo is about to be original. Beware, claiming originality is open for very personal interpretations, but using unique techniques and developing a unique idea can be taken as the original. For instance, an image that carries a story, a history, or an identity, etc. War photography specifically springs to mind as an example.

Good photography is also putting things and images together in a skillful way. Photography is a somewhat acceptable type of creativity that enables endless flexibility in the way you adapt it to your style. A well-trained photographer should emember that another important idea for an ideal photograph is clicking the most suitable picture at the proper time. For instance, if you are after a stunning sunset, timing and planning is everything.

For the first impression, it's the overall beauty and the unique perspective that catches the gaze of the viewer. The clarity, precision, balance, and exclusive quality of the picture is the next step one should consider. The third step is to critically observe errors and good qualities. The fourth step is to analyze the techniques and camera settings that are used to take the picture and what other settings could be used for better results. The last step is to grade the picture with fair remarks.

What's next? Go out there and keep shooting.

The Genres of Photography

- **Landscape**. Landscape photography captures the vast, unending spaces, and sometimes microscopic views. Landscape usually shoots the manifestation of nature, but it also can be human-made features. There are several essential factors behind the importance of landscape photography. The most important among them is outdoor experience and personal observation while traveling. Landscape photographs are photographed in the pursuit of the pure, immaculate depiction of nature, devoid of human influence or human presence. Landscape photography is the broader form of art that may include rural and urban settings of nature photography.
- **Architecture Photography**. Architecture photography also denoted as the structure photography or building photography taken as the most important and historical genre of photography. It mainly focuses on shooting buildings, interiors and exteriors, bridges, structures, and cityscapes. The street art photography also focuses on shooting the beauty of famous and historical buildings captured in a way that is aesthetically pleasing while having the precise illustration of their subjects.
- **Portraiture Photography**. Portrait photography is about capturing a person in a way that enhances the essence of a person's identity, attitude,

and personality. The in-depth of portraiture photography involves the unique skills of the photographer to craft a photograph of a person's face distinguishing the facial features. Portrait photography is about the background, person's dressing, position, and angle of the photo are prepared before the actual photo-shoot takes place.

- **Photojournalism.** Photojournalism is one of the most exciting genres of the art of photography. Every object captured by the eye of a camera has a story and deep meanings hidden inside. Photojournalism is one shot to a whole story. One single photo tells the entire narrative. Photojournalists are smart enough to capture to shoot photos talking about social injustice.
- **Wildlife and Nature Photography.** Nature photography requires a creative eye to capture the aesthetic beauty of nature, sometimes called garden photography, wildlife photography, and landscape photography. Nature never forgets to amaze us with its magnificent scenery, nor does the photograph that captures it fully. Wildlife and nature photography don't offer the conventional ground as studio photography, as it always demands unusual angle and focus. Studio photography requires variety by using traditional techniques, while wildlife and nature photography demands a unique stance out of unique camera settings.
- **Sports Photography.** Sports photography holds the professional ground to capture passion, devotion, and goals in the field. The moment of victory and the moment of failure are worth capturing memories in the scrapbook called that can be worth entitling "the road to success."
- **Still Life Photography**. Still, life photography captures the ordinary and uninteresting objects in a way that makes them unique together in one photograph. What makes a fruit basket or empty glass bottles so interesting? Through a unique angle, lighting, and composition, still, life experts can breathe life into ordinary objects.
- **Fashion Photography.** Fashion photography is one of the most expensive photography capturing the fashion aesthetics of the fast-paced world of fashion. It encircles around on portraiture, extensive lighting, posing, and

beautiful locations. The genre is continuously evolving and changing, along with trends.

TIP: what photography genre interests you the most? I would advise to start focusing one 1-2 genres at first because it will help you to strengthen on the technique that matters the most. As you go along with photography, you will slowly learn how to translate your skill set to any other genre.

The Skills to Capture

The human eyes see the world in little chunks, put together to form a picture. The angle of the sharp vision of the human eye is tremendously tiny- just three radial degrees. The human eye sees in small sharp bits, and extremely fast to view the entire scene.

The most exciting fact is, the human eye doesn't collect images categorically or doesn't see the scene with uniform sharpness or interest. The art of proper composition is the artist's way of leading the viewer's vision in a planned and non-random fashion. Through the composition, the photographer brings order to the non-ordered world.

For beginners, simplicity is essential. The simplified composition is to have control and to capture some crucial elements. The control and caption would grow more experienced and sophisticated for complex situations at advanced level composition. The simplified composition elucidates the photographer's thoughts clearly and precisely. While complex composition often lacks clarity and precision.

Photography is also the skill of the right or the right moment. Landscape photographers spend days and nights, even years, for the moment to catch. The right time and right actions make the picture-perfect image.

Perfect Imperfect

To analyze the perfection of a picture, one can see the story, twist, quality, and technically as good as possible. A question emerges that does a good picture can be made with the right amount of composition, exposure, and focus? In photojournalism it's not necessary. Any blurred, out of focus, and underexposed image can be received as the most precious pictures for the importance of event and narrative it captures. The pictures of World War I and II are taken as valuable sources that depict the destruction at a grand scale the world ever witnessed. The photographs of all historical events, movements, and revolutions are stored as the token of national identities. These pictures are priceless, but if they get auctioned, they will earn the highest bids ever collected on any masterpiece of art.

Rule of Thirds

There are several composition "rules" in photography to help to create harmony between your subject and the scene. One of the most commonly used is the "rule o thirds". It is a simple and easy concept that breaks the image into 9 equal squares. The important compositional elements are then placed along these lines or their intersections to give your image a sense of flow, depth, and balance. It's a good way of adding complexity to the image rather than just putting the subject at the center Let's look at same examples:

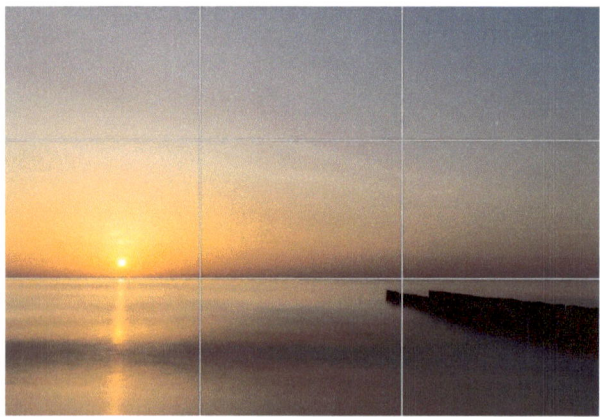

The horizon is placed along one of the horizontal lines, whereas the main subject is at the lowest intersection (Photography © Fabrizio Micciche)

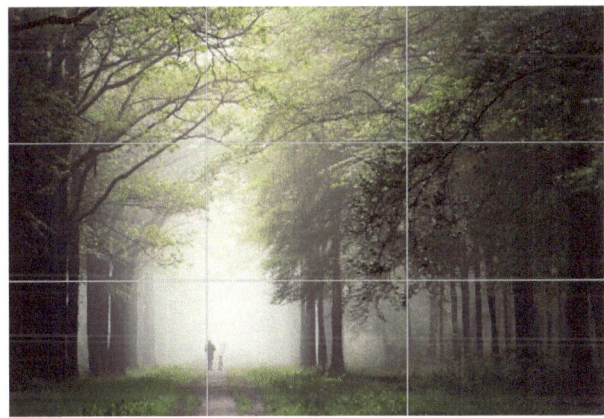

The subject was placed at the left, bottom intercept to create a balance in the composition. (Photography © Fabrizio Micciche)

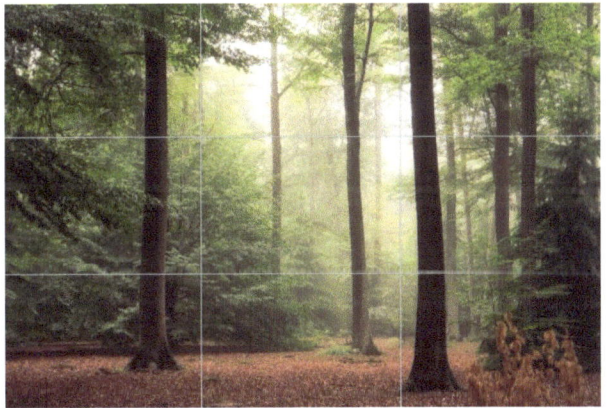

Another example of rule of thirds but this time not a specific subject but on the backlight. (Photography © Fabrizio Micciche)

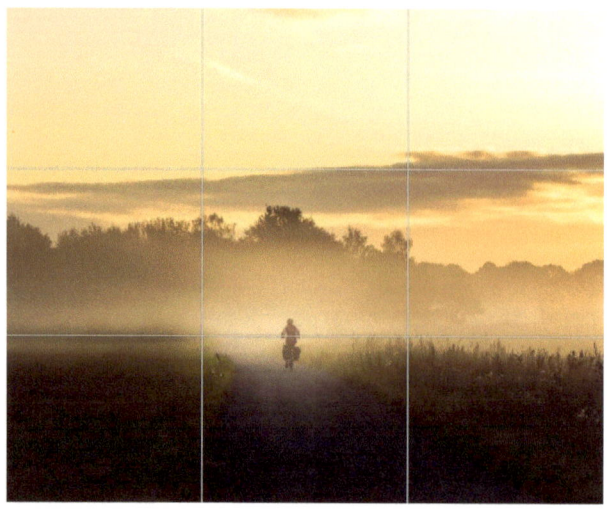

The exception to the rule. In this image I thought that placing the subject to the center would draw the viewer straight into the mist (Photography © Fabrizio Micciche)

TIP: How to see the grid in your camera? Typically, you can have them appearing in the screen when in live view. Remember that the rules of thirds, like the others, are more compositional guidance than exact rules to be followed. Experiment with positioning a subject on the different intersections and then in the center. What is the most balanced/appealing photo(s)? Ask for an opinion on a non-photographer to see how they feel the various images.

Anatomy of DSLR

The anatomy of the digital single-lens reflex camera (digital SLR or DSLR) consists of two parts; the body and the lens. The body contains all the necessary control, digital processing elements and features that allow us to capture an image. Different cameras and camera manufacture might structure all these elements in various layouts depending on the model of the camera. Nevertheless, some features are common to whatever brand and camera type including, but not limited to, shutter release button, aperture control wheel, sensor, mode wheel, viewfinder, LCD screen, media card door, and battery access. Additional features including body design to grip and handle easily might vary depending on the brand of your camera.

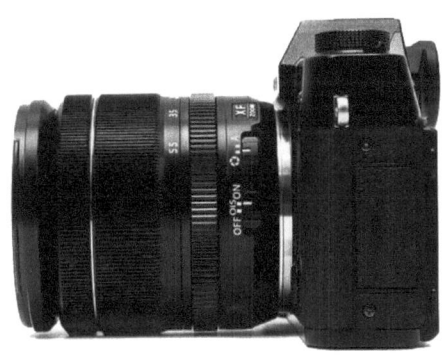

TIP: *take some time to explore and get to know your camera. Learn what buttons and commands are available at your fingertip. Get familiar with the menu and some of the options your camera has to offer.*

Coming to the lens, it consists of lens cap\hood\filter, glass- multiple lens elements, aperture\focus\zoom ring, auto\manual switch, distance indicator, DOP indicator, image stabilization controls, and lens mount. Similarly, to the camera body, the quality of the glass used into a lens and the various auto and manual controlled modes vary from manufacture to manufacture.

Viewfinder

The viewfinder in modern digital cameras is the little rectangle window on top of your camera where you look at the view you wish to capture. It helps you to analyze and compose the scene. Typically, it shows important information about the camera settings such as Aperture, Shutter, ISO, Exposure and Focus point(s).

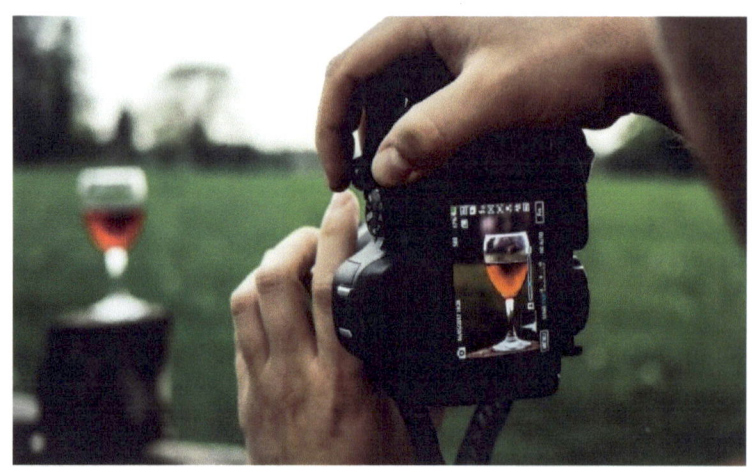

Photo by Jamie Street, Focal Length 20 mm, ISO 200, Aperture f/1.7, Shutter Speed 1/1250 sec

Viewfinders can be either optical or electronic. DSLRs have an optical TTL (through the lens) viewfinder, which allows you to look through the lens and see precisely what the lens projects onto the sensor. Electronic or digital viewfinders are usually the LCD screen on the back of the DSLR. The LCD screen can be used to review photos, compose your image and also displays the camera's menus, features, focus points and functions. This is also known as "live view".

Holding your camera

The first step of learning photography is to keep your camera balanced to avoid blurry images. Shooting a good picture with a super-focused vision requires handholding the camera steadily. Keep the camera in the handgrip of your right hand support the lens so that it will help to balance the weight of the camera. Place your elbows slightly held against your torso for support. To maintain the balance, keep one foot slightly ahead of another. Composing the frame shot through the viewfinder and gently press the shutter release button.

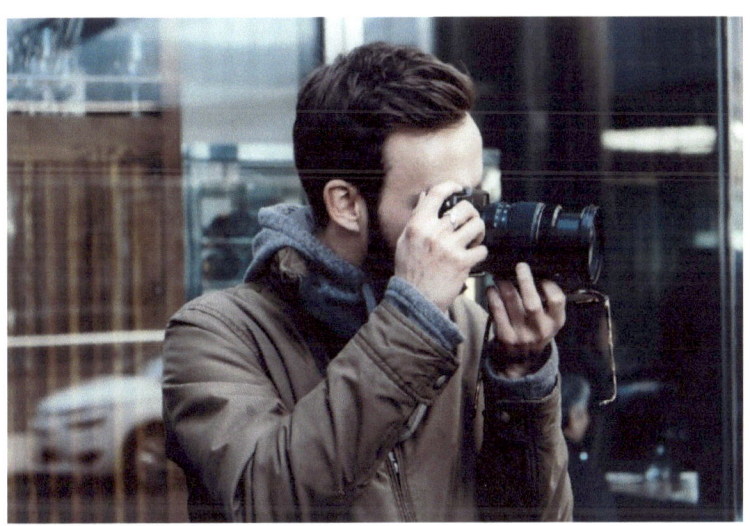

Photo by Annie Spratt, Focal Length 55 mm, ISO 320, Aperture f/4.0, Shutter Speed 1/100 sec

For beginners, learning photography can be frustrating when you find controlling hand-shakes and blurry photos. Keeping the camera as steady as possible is one of the mastering skills of photography. You will have to practice a lot with holding your camera steady and getting crisp and clear shots.

One also can use equipment like a tripod or a lens and/or camera built-in vibration reduction (VR) to get a balanced, focused, stabilized image. Tripod is the best support to get steady pictures. Things to avoid in order to grasp your camera correctly

- Don't hold your camera in only one hand
- Spreading your both elbows apart will reduce the stability of the hold. Keep your elbows in a way that helps you maintain the steadiness and better grip on the camera

- Don't leave your lens unsupported
- Don't grip your lens too loosely

TIP: *learn how to hold your camera is very important. Spend some time to feel and touch your camera for the best and most comfortable holding technique that suits you. If you have multiple lenses, change your lens and try again. Using a small or a big lens will require you to change how to efficiently hold your camera.*

Depending on your posture when taking the photo, you might need to adjust your holding technique accordingly. Here are some suggestions.

- **Crouching.** Taking the caption while crouching will help you make a photograph from different angles. For this, you need to maintain the perfect balance for squatting position. Don't crouch in a way that leaves your elbows unsupported. Keep your both elbows on your knees so you can have enough support to avoid the handshake and blur.
- **Standing.** While standing, keep your legs a little apart to have the balance Closing together, your legs will look like tense and unsteady stance.
- **Sitting.** Most of the time, photographs don't involve a sitting position, but if you do, it is better to keep your legs a little apart to maintain the balance To support your elbows, keep your knees under your elbows. Don't sit in the position when your feet don't have a firm position.
- **Lying Down.** Lying down position reminds us about the photographers lying among the bushes over the hill having the cameras focused on animals or any other subject. Lying down position helps you to get the most interesting and "worm's eye" view of the world. However maintaining the balance and holding your camera steady is still very essential. Keep yourself supported with your elbows.

JPEG vs. RAW

In photography, the RAW format is the unprocessed, uncooked, raw data collected from the scene by the camera sensor. A RAW file is a big size format file, in which image records most of the information from the camera without processing and compression. Often it does not look appealing but it has enormous potential in what you can achieve with it and contains all the necessary information to process and edit your photos.

JPEG, on the other hand, is the final product. When you apply a series of edits to your RAW image and are happy with the result, you save it to your portfolio in JPEG format. That's it. It looks beautiful but there is no way back. JPEG file is a standard image format small file size in which information processed and compressed. It is a very common image format, easy to open, compression level quality, easy to use, and convenient.

While most of the professional photographers insist on using RAW format because of a few favorable reasons and advantages of RAW file format so, the question arises why we should use or choose RAW format rather than another file format or JPEG? The reason to use RAW is that one can process the image by his\herself, highest quality, best brightness as JPEG captures in 8 bit, and RAW is either 12bit or 14bit, correct dramatically over/underexposed images, control white balance with better detail, and effective workflow without a drastic reduction in quality. As a photographer, working with RAW files is the rule rather than the exception.

TIP: often, I should in both RAW and JPEG at the same time. Why? Because I let the camera work out my photos to have a feeling on the potential final look of the final shot. Another advantage is that previewing JPEG images in your PC will be faster than RAW files especially if you wish to go through dozens of shots quickly. Nevertheless, shooting RAW remains your first priority.

Light in photography

Light is the true source behind the vivid beauty of the shot. It's the light that plays the central part in enhancing the creative mode of photography. There are four controllable qualities of light that are intensity, color, direction, and movement. Lighting is key to the effective development of a photograph. Brightness, darkness, tone, mood, and atmosphere of the image are determined by lighting. Through positioning, shaping, manipulating light, one can control texture, vibrancy, and luminosity of subjects. Natural light always becomes the best choice while capturing photographs as it produces depth and avoids shadows. However, there are situations where artificial lights, reflectors, and flash are handy especially while shooting in studios.

Explaining Color Temperature

Light sources produce different colored light. These different colors expressed in Kelvins, symbol K, a unit of measure for absolute temperature, and this number is known as the color temperature. Soft white 2700K – 3000K, bright white/cool white 3500K – 4100K, and daylight 5000K – 6500K are the primary range of color distinguished as cool and warm colors temperature. Higher the numbers, the cooler the temperature will be.

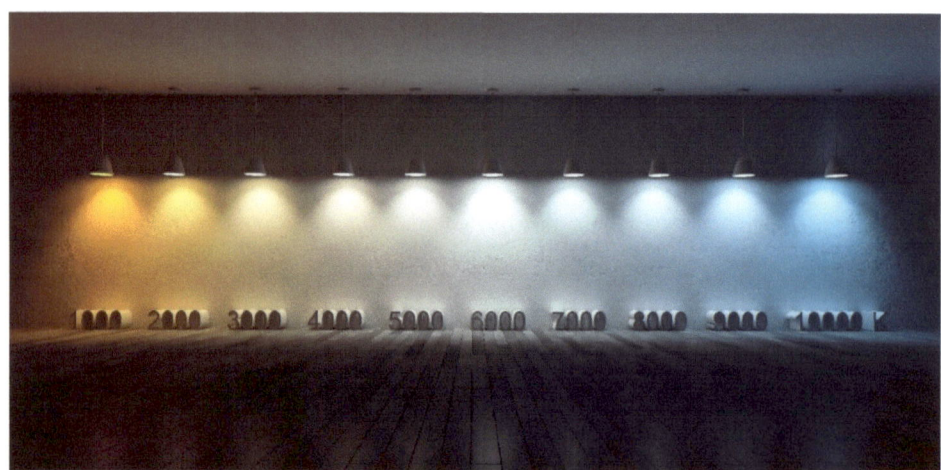

White Balance

In photography and image processing, white balance is the adjustment of colors so that the image looks more natural. Selecting the correct white balance by observing the light temperature (in Kelvin) of the scene to change the tone or impact of your images. You can set it to automatic on your camera or tweak it depending on the tone you want to achieve. When you set your camera's white balance manually you can choose from a number of pre-set color temperature options like Daylight, Cloudy, and Shade, or customize your own setting.

TIP: what white balance setting to use? Typically, I would start in automatic mode because it works quite well. However, I would encourage you to try to use the closest withe balance setting that fits the light you're shooting at. Are you at the beach shooting at sunset? Try to take three shots: one with Daylight, one with Shade and the other with Cloudy white balance. What to expect? Warmer images as you move from day to cloudy. See what image is closer to the original scene and works best for you.

Camera Lenses Explained

Introducing Lenses

The camera lenses are one of the essential parts of the camera. The quality of shots and images highly depends on the careful selection of lenses. For the selection of a suitable lens, you need to research on several important factors such as its ideal focal length, speed, compatibility with the camera, and your budget.

A lens draws light onto the sensor of the camera, which is critical to photography. Lens affects the quality of a photo through focal length, aperture, maximum aperture, and DOF (depth of field). Before we move further, let's discuss the varieties of lens lets and understand focal length.

Understanding Digital Photography

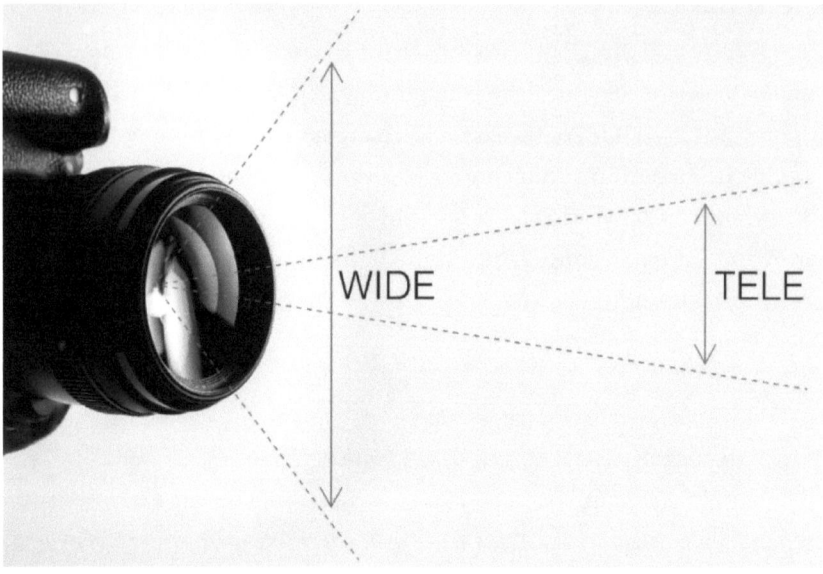

When light enters the camera, that light makes a crossing point known as a center point or nodal point. The area or distance from the center point to the imaging sensor is known as the focal length. Smaller numbers have a wider angle of view and show more of the scene, and long focal length creates narrow angles as in the telephoto lens.

Type and variety of lenses existing and their focal length:

- **Prime Lenses**. Prime lenses have no zoom in or zoom out with fixed focal length to capture crisp and sharp images. They are fast and light-weighted but not flexible.
- **Zoom Lenses**. Zoom lenses have an adjustable focal length and have a series of lenses to allow different focal lengths from a single lens. It is flexible but not fast. It can be zoomed from moderate wide-angle, from average to extreme wide-angle lens, and from usual to intense telephoto. It has the focal length up to 18–55–100 mm.
- **Ultra-wide angle (focal length 8 mm to 24 mm)**. These lenses are sometimes called fisheye lenses, which have a very wide viewing area.

While they can take an image of up to 180 degrees around the lens, they distort the image quite significantly, making everything appear almost as if inside a sphere.
- **Standard Wide-Angle lenses (focal length 24 mm to 35 mm).** Wide-Angle lenses capture more of the scene having the focal length starting from 24mm or less. Landscape, a massive waterfall, and street photography are examples of wide-angle lenses. The wide-angle lens falls furthermore into rectilinear and fisheye (keep the proportion and perspective as accurate to reality.)
- **Standard lens (focal length 35 mm to 70 mm).** A standard lens is inexpensive and easy to design. It captures varieties of views that are visible to the human eye or which appears natural. A standard lens has a focal length of 42mm on a full-frame camera with a high focus on the view. Produces versatile, excellent image quality, and the optical quality is superb. Its wide aperture gives the ability to make a bokeh effect (blur background). It has a static focal length up to (50mm, 85mm, and 100mm)
- **Telephoto lenses (focal length 70 mm to 300 mm or more).** Telephoto lenses are a zoom type with several focal points. They usually are longer than 70 mm brings scenes and objects closer to the photographer (isolating a subject that is far away). To capture sports scenes and actions, a telephoto lens is the best suggestion to offer.
- **Portrait lenses.** A focal lens of 85 to 135 mm with a fast aperture, is conventional for shooting portraits.
- **Macro.** This kind of camera lens is used to create macro photographs at an extremely close range. The focal length of the macro lens is great for nature photography. It has to power to produces an enormous amount of detail in one image.

How to Choose Your First Lens

For starters, I would strongly recommend a basic set of lenses that allow you to over various photography genre. There is a good chance that your camera came with kit lens. Therefore, the question we need to ask ourselves is what do we gain by buying a second lens? If you're into flower or insect photography, you might want to look at a macro lens. If the landscape is your passion, you might be looking for a wide angle lens. What about wildlife? Then a telephoto lens is what you need to get you a closer look. Is portrait your passion? An 85 mm lens is the way to go even though it might be a bit expensive.

When I first started with photography, I had a very tight budget to spare for a new camera and lenses. So, I had considered and re-consider a couple of times before going to the shop and buy my gear. This is what I ended up with:

- **Nikon D3100.** This is an entry-level 14.2-megapixel DX-format DSLR Nikon capable of great image quality, full HD video recording capabilities and a solid autofocus system. It is a small and easy-to-handle camera and it comes with the 18-55 mm kit lens. Was I happy? Yes, very much because I capture fantastic shots with it. This camera is no longer in production and it has been replaced with the D3300. There are tons of great entry-level cameras you can choose from.
- **a 50 mm, f/1.8 primes lens.** It is inexpensive, sharp, lightweight and thanks to its f/1.8 aperture it gives lots of flexibility to shoot under low light condition and it delivers excellent stand out portraits.
- **18-105 mm, f/3.5-5**. Although it has a variable aperture depending on the focal length, this is a great all-around lens that will give you a wide view at 18 mm, and the ability to zoom in on your subject.

As I advanced in photography my needs started to change and so was the technical specs I was after. I slowly added a new camera, a wide-angle lens, another prime (35 mm, f/1.4) and the fantastic 70-200 mm, f/2.8. Please be aware that many photographers have varying opinions on what lens is the best for every situation. What I suggest is my personal opinion and personal preference.

> **TIP:** *there are many different lenses out there. What lens will you use? Photography might easily become a costly hobby unless you really focus on the gear you actually need. Be aware to not get trapped into G.A.S. (Gear Acquisition Syndrome)! If you wish try new gears opt for the rent and/or borrow option first. Better spend your time into education than thousands of dollars in gears you actually do not need.*

It is worth mentioning that a lot of professional photographers need certain equipment for certain tasks. If you are a fashion photographer and going to print out billboard-sized prints, it is preferable to have a medium-format camera. But if you are a hobbyist or a starter, you surely don't need 40+ megapixels. Don't convince yourself that you "need" something, especially if you can't afford it. Remember, a camera is a tool needed to perform a task and its monetary value does not imply better photography. First, explore, try, make mistakes and be creative. What to buy next will come naturally.

Chapter 2: Understanding Aperture

What is the Focal Length? Focal length, generally described in millimeters (mm), is the primary information of the camera lens. It is not an estimation of the actual length of a lens. It's a measurement of an apparent distance from the position where light rays intersect to create a sharp caption of the subject to the camera's sensor at the focal length. The focal length of a lens is measured when the lens is centered at infinity. The focal length of the lens determines how 'zoomed in' your photos are. The higher the number, the more your lens will be able to zoom into the scene. Later we will learn how lenses are classified based on their focal length characteristics. If we look inside a camera lens and we shine a light at the proper angle, you'll see something that looks like this:

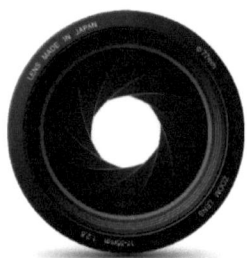

The elements present at the center of the lens are called blades that form a small hole, almost circular in shape. Welcome to the world of "aperture". Often, you'll hear other photographers talking about large versus small apertures. They will tell you to "stop down" (close) or "open up" (widen) the aperture blades to photograph to accomplish a certain effect under the available light.

There are differences between photos taken with a large aperture versus photos taken with a small aperture.

Aperture size has a direct impact on the brightness of a photograph. Larger apertures let in more light into the camera compared to smaller apertures. However, that isn't the only thing that aperture affects. One of them is called "depth of field". This determines the amount of your photo that appears to be sharp from front to back. Let's consider the illustrations below. By changing how wide the blades of your lens are (aperture) you basically change the depths of field of the final image.

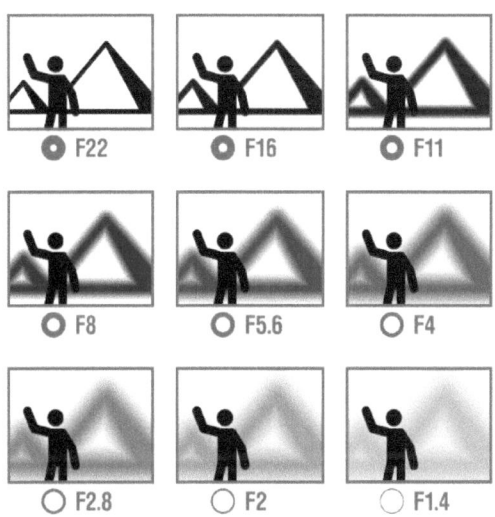

Adjusting your aperture is one of the best tools you have to capture the right images. You can adjust it by entering your camera's aperture-priority mode or manual mode. As you advance in photography you will get more familiar with both modes you will empower yourself to full controlling your camera. In other words, by changing your lens aperture, you shape up the feel and look of your shots.

What is f-stop?

As a beginner photographer, you might have heard the terms **f-stop** or **f-number** and wondered what they actually mean. In simple words, the f-stop is the number that your camera shows you when you change the size of the lens aperture. The "f" stands for focal length and on your camera's LCD screen or viewfinder, the f-stop looks like f/1.2, f/2.8, f/4, f/5.6, f/8, f/11, and so on. Each number corresponds to a certain diameter at the center of your lens as depicted below. Sometimes, it will be shown without a slash in between like f2.8, or with a capital "F" letter in the front like F2.8.

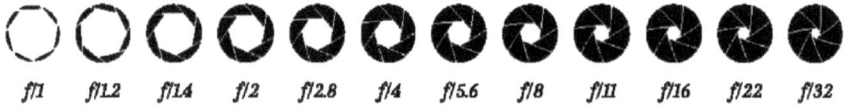

f/1   f/1.2   f/1.4   f/2   f/2.8   f/4   f/5.6   f/8   f/11   f/16   f/22   f/32

It is important to understand that a certain lens will be capable of delivering a certain minimum and maximum f-stop. This means that the lens blades will not be able to open or close any further. Why caring so much about the maximum aperture a lens can offer? Essentially because lens with a larger maximum aperture will allow more light to reach the camera sensor. These are also called fast lens. For example, in a lens with a maximum aperture of f/2.8 enters twice as much light when compared to a lens with a maximum aperture of f/4.0. This is a significant difference when shooting in low-light conditions or when you wish to have greater control over the depth of field and thereof isolation of your subject in your image.

TIP: start practicing with the f-stops and depth of field with simple scenes. You could, for instance, choose a tree at your front doorstep, place a glass on a table or use a friend as a model in your backyard.

Mastering aperture via either the manual mode or aperture priority mode of your camera is key to control your aperture instead of letting your camera doing it for you. This is a crucial starting point to the essential creative decisions that will make your photograph to look better. The level of aperture, of f-stop, you choose can be classified in the three main categories and each having some important features.

- **Wide Aperture.** The wide aperture reduces the depth of the field. Only your focus point would look sharp, and almost everything will be blurred in the background. It is one of the efficient techniques to conceal the background completely. Think about a portrait photo where you wish to have your subject standing out and well separated from the background. The f-stop would be below f/4 and ideally f/2.8 or below for even more separation between the subject and the background.
- **Medium Aperture.** It delivers a balanced light through the lens to provide the best performance of the image to capture the sharpness of the focus point and background. Medium aperture draws a perfect balance between the light and the depth of the field. The f-stop would be f/5.6 and f/8.
- **Small Aperture.** Small aperture allows the minimum light at an f-stop of f/11 and higher. It decreases the amount of light passing through the camera's lens and enhances the depth of the field to the maximum. It covers the maximum scene in the sharp focus. A small aperture is the best technique when you want to focus everything on the view such as a landscape.

Shooting in Aperture Priority Mode

Aperture priority mode is a very handy semi-auto dial mode, often abbreviated A or Av (for aperture value), on your camera. It allows you to set a specific aperture value (f-number) while letting the camera selecting a proper shutter speed to properly expose based on the available lighting conditions as measured by the camera's light meter. If the light conditions are more on the shadow/dark side, be aware that the shutter speed might drop below a value that can result in motion blur. So just keep an eye on your camera settings. Increase your ISO if you need to compensate and increase your shutter speed. Let's walk through two assignments to master shooting in Aperture Priority Mode. First thing first: look for A or Av on your camera. Typically this is present as one of the options on the small wheel on top of your camera body. You are ready to start shooting.

Exercise 1: Keeping Everything in Focus

Let's image you are on top of a stunning mountain and you wish to capture the stunning view before you such to keep the entire scene as sharp as your human eye can see it.

1: Set Aperture. To maintain the whole scene sharp, front to end, adjust the aperture at f/8-f/11.

2: Check Shutter Speed. Based on the aperture you choose, the appropriate shutter speed will be automatically decided by your camera. In general, the minimum handheld shutter speed is the reciprocal of the focal length of the lens. So, if you're using a 100 mm lens (bear in mind any crop factor) then the slowest shutter speed you should try and use is 1/100th of a second. In other words, if your focal length is 100 mm, your shutter speed needs to be at least 1/100 sec. This rule does not always work especially, though. If your shutter speed is below 1/100 sec, it can be a bit too slow to take sharp photos handheld. Consider either are increasing your ISO (= faster shutter speeds) or a tripod.

3: Review the Image. After taking the first image, carefully analyze the depth field and the focused image. Use the camera's playback zoom controls to zoom-in and zoom out to have a detailed review of the depth of the field. Scroll around the photos to see the farthest and nearest areas of your captions.

Exercise 2: Using Shallow Depth of Field for Portraits

Using of wide aperture for portraiture photography is one of the traditional and creative arts of maximizing the image's impact. In portrait photography, the object of focus is more important than the background. It is essential to draw the viewer's attention towards the subject by reducing the other distractions in the background. The most impactful results are obtained using (fast) lenses with an f-number of f/2.8 and below.

1. Position Your Subject. If you want to shoot a close-up portrait, you need to make your subject positioned a little away from the background and zoom-in to cover the frame. It is a more practical technique to get a reduced depth of field and to get a close focus on the subject.

2. Select Wide Aperture. A wide aperture means to choose small f-number like f/1.8-f/4 to get the shallow depth of the field. The prime lenses have the maximized wide apertures than the zoom lenses.

3. Select the Focus Point. Focus on your subject, steady-hold your camera and when you are happy with the composition, press the shutter speed.

Chapter 3: Learning and Understanding Shutter Speed

The shutter speed is one of the essential factors that change the brightness of your photo and allows modifying the depth of focus and the sharpness of the subject including freezing action or blurring motion. Essentially it's how long your camera spends taking a photo. Shutter speed is most commonly measured in fractions of a second, like 1/200 seconds or 1/1000 seconds. Some high-end cameras offer shutter speeds as fast as 1/8000 seconds.

Shutter speeds can extend to much longer times, generally up to 30 seconds on most cameras. That time can be prolonged further into minutes or even hours by using the so-called Bulb Mode, which is denoted with a B in your camera's menu system and gives you many creative options for using shutter speed.

Another important effect the shutter speed has is on the overall exposure. If you use long shutter speed, your camera will spend a long time taking the image allowing lots of light to reach the camera sensor. The result is bright photos. On the contrary, by using fast shutter speed, your camera sensor is exposed to light for a small fraction of a second, resulting in darker photos. Therefore, changing your shutter speed will also require to properly balance the aperture to balance the overall exposure. Later on, we will learn another parameter called ISO that will help you balancing everything together.

Fast shutter speeds are used to freeze motion and eliminate the motion of fast-moving subjects. Think about a fast speeding car, your kids running around or a bird flying on the sky. There is a significant difference between a sharp photo and a slightly blurred image.

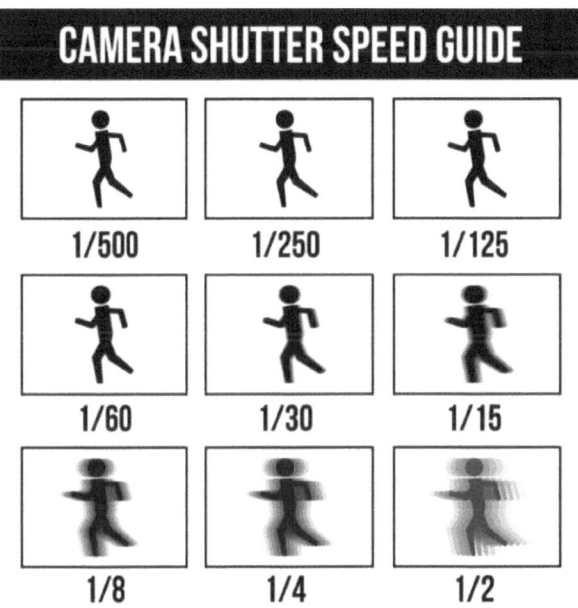

The moving branches of trees, flowing water, people walking in the street are the examples for the mild movements that can be brought into sharp focus by adjusting the shutter speed. On the contrary long shutter speeds introduce the so-called motion blur. A common example is giving by the silky appearance of fast running water or to photograph the milky way at night. Be aware that the longer the shutter speeds, the greater the stabilization your camera needs. Therefore, if long exposure is a type of photography you are interested into, I'd advise to invest in a good tripod. An example of long exposure image is given below. See how interesting and smooth the sea looks?

TIP: I am personally fascinated by long exposure photography. Try to shoot at the beach at sunset at ISO 100, f/8-9 such to reach shutter speed of a few seconds. The scene will be transformed into something magical. Try any range to see what motion blur can or can't do for you.

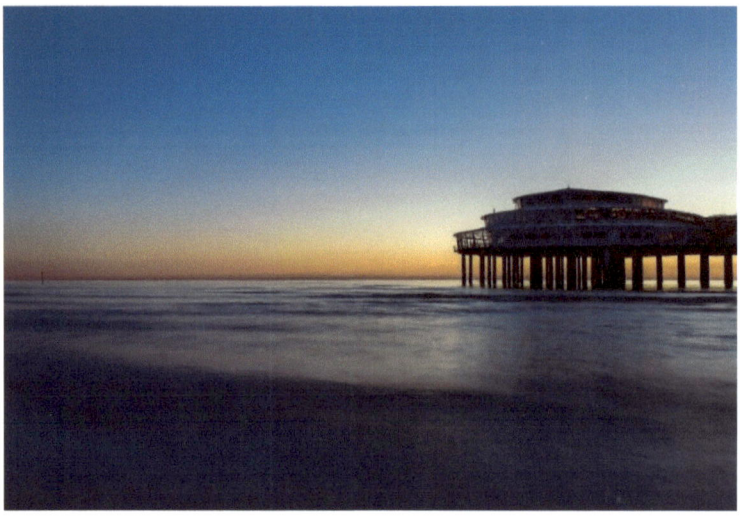

Photo by Fabrizio Micciche, Focal Length 20 mm, ISO 100, Aperture f/9, Shutter Speed 2.6 sec

Here's a few suggested shutter speeds for different subjects:

- **Sports Photography.** Sports photography requires the freezing of the particular movement of the player. It's related to high-impact and freeze-images of players captioned at the highest peak of their actions. You can choose the minimum speed 1/500 to freeze motion or 1/60 sec to introduce partial blur to the moments.
- **Light Trails**. Light trails are one of the best ways to add a wow factor to your urban night photography. Traffic and car light trails add lots of interesting lights and elements in your cityscapes. Typical settings are: lowest ISO possible (typically 100-200), aperture between f/5.6-11, shutter speed between 10 and 30 sec. A good and stable tripod is needed.
- **Wildlife**. In this case precision and speed are everything. To get the desired focus on moving animals, highlighting textures, you need to extend the exposure time to caption more creative images of the natural aesthetics.

The suggested shutter speed is a minimum 1/2000 to freeze and 1/125 sec to blur the wildlife moment.
- **Water.** Photographing water allows you to boost your creativity to anything you like. Opt for fast shutter speeds to freeze motion, such a big wave at the beach. Or stretch your shutter speeds to seconds or even minutes to give it that special silky look. Shoot pin-sharp droplets of water, gushing waves or murky water can lead to incredibly beautiful, dramatic and ethereal feel. The suggested shutter speed is a minimum of 1/1000 to freeze and up to a few seconds to blur the water.

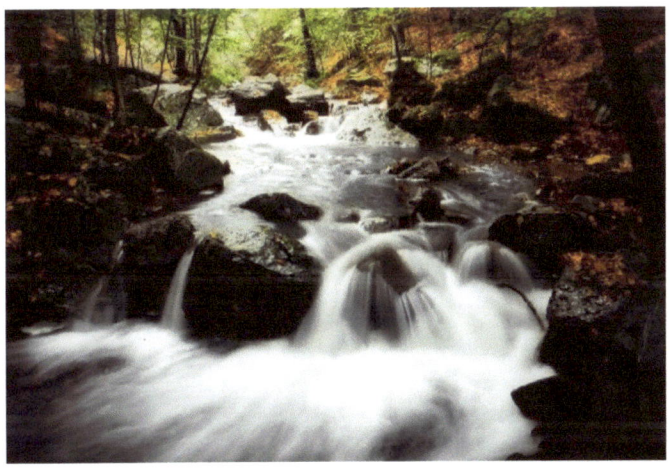

Photo by Fabrizio Micciche, Focal Length 20 mm, ISO 100, Aperture f/9, Shutter Speed 0.8 sec

Exercise 3: Free motion with the fast shutter speed

Let's suppose that you wish to capture a stunning photo of your dog running like the one in the image. Assuming that you are in full daylight and need a shutter speed of 1/1000 this is how to proceed.

Understanding Digital Photography

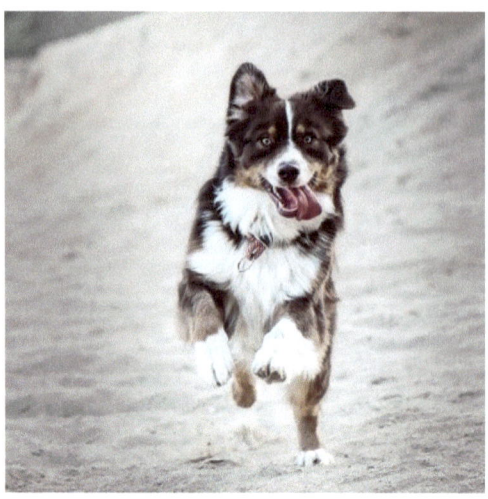

Photo by Joséphine Menge, aperture f/2.8, ISO 400, shutter speed 1/1000 sec, focal length 90 mm

1. **Choose Shutter Priority Mode**. Choose the shutter priority on your camera to get more control over the shutter speed
2. **Adjustment of Shutter Speed**. Our goal is to freeze motion, so let start with dialing in a 1/1000 second shutter speed
3. **ISO.** Since we are in full daylight, let's set the ISO to 100-200
4. **Frame Your Shot**. First, looking around, choosing the best viewpoint, and careful attention to background to get the best view along with the background scenery.
5. **Shooting.** When you press the shutter button, the camera will determine the aperture that's needed to get a well-exposed image given the shutter speed
6. **Optional:** Activate Continuous Shooting Drive. By turning this mode on will allow you to have increased numbers of exposures in rapid succession so you choose the best later.
7.

Fabrizio Miccichè

Exercise 4: Silky water with slow shutter speed

Slow shutter speeds can also be used intentionally to blur the image. By matching the shutter speed with medium or small aperture priority mode to reduce the amount of passing light. For this situation, you can also keep ISO low to being with the best start.

1. **Adjust Your Tripod.** Tripod is the best tool to capture images at a slow shutter speed to avoid camera shakes. Make sure to have stable legs on a stable position.
2. **Frame your shot.** Since you are on a tripod, I would advise you to turn on the live view mode of your camera. Frame your shot to give the best composition and balance within the elements. You might consider applying the rule of thirds (see page xx).
3. **Choose Shutter Priority Mode.** How slow would you shoot? I would start from a shutter speed of 0.8 – 1.0 sec. Not silky enough? Go slower but try to stay below 2.5 - 3.0 sec unless you would like to hide any sort of structure. If after fixing your aperture to e.g. f/8-10 you cannot get the slow speed you need, it means that there is too much light. Consider to go back either early morning or late afternoon when the light is milder. If long exposure is your passion, consider to invest in neutral density filters (not covered in this book).
4. **Self-timer.** Set a delay of 10 sec between the moment you hit the shutter-release button and moment your camera takes the shoot. This will ensure that no camera shakes are present during the shoot. For super slow speed, a remote release is handy to have.
5. **Select an Autofocus Point.** If you are in live view mode, you will manually need to select where to focus. To maintain the whole scene sharp, a rule of thumb is to focus at 1/3 of your frame. Remember the rule of thirds and how we subdivide the scene into 9 equal squares? This included 3 main horizontal lines. Focusing at 1/3 of your frame would equal to place your focus point anywhere along the first line (from the bottom). As an

alternative, you can turn the live view off and let your camera focus automatically via the viewfinder.

6. **Shooting.** Happy with all your settings? Half-press the shutter speed to allow the camera to autofocus. Then press it all the way done gently, take your hands off the camera and wait for the shooting to happen.

Exercise 5: Panning for Sharpness and Blur

To get both freezing and blurring in your image is easily attainable. The moving object appears as sharp as it seems, while the surrounding background is blurry. This is called panning and an example is giving below.

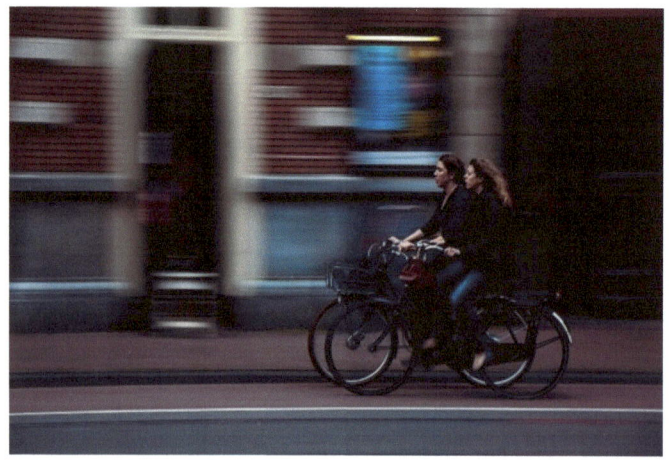

Photo by Davic Marcu, aperture f/5.3, ISO 320, shutter speed 1/15 sec, focal length 70 mm

1. **Frame your shot.** Frame your shot to give the best composition and balance within the elements. You might consider applying the rule of thirds.
2. **Choose the Shutter Priority Mode.** For the best start, select the 1/60 sec shutter speed.
3. **Image Stabilization.** Without the tripod, it is better to turn on the image stabilization of your lens if available to avoid the shakes. You should avail of the benefits of this feature if you have it on your camera. If extra

stabilization is not available, no panic! This is a good moment to practice and master how to hold the camera steady.
4. **Choose Continuous Autofocus.** For the fast-moving objects, selecting the continuous autofocus mode as the camera will compensate for a motion to keep your subject look sharp and clear.
5. **Pan the Camera.** Follow your subject with your camera via the viewfinder. Keep an eye on the place that you want your subject to be. When there, press the shutter-release.

This is a more advance technique that requires some experience. So, keep on trying ill you get the result you want.

Chapter 4: Introducing ISO

ISO is one of the primary features that brightens or darkens your image. Increasing ISO numbers mean brighter pictures, and it will help you in taking photographs in a dark environment and at night. Nevertheless, increasing the ISO number has some drawbacks that need to be avoided. At too high ISO, lots of grains will show on the photo. Capturing the picture at high ISO will produce the so called color and light noise. See the image below as an example. It is recommended to start increasing your ISO only in the circumstances when you cannot brighten the photos with the help of aperture and shutter speed settings. The lowest ISO value begins with the number ISO 100, and the most common highest is ISO 6400. However, the highest value will strongly depend on your camera as it can go as high as 20000 and above.

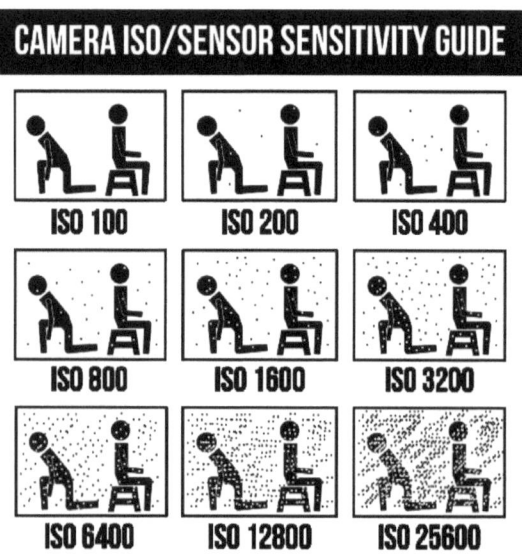

When to Use Low or High ISO

Using the lowest ISO all the time when taking a photograph is normal. When there is sufficient light, you can use the lower number value of ISO, which is the modern camera 100. If you are shooting in shady or dark environments and you are using a tripod, remember that you can brighten the picture by long shutter speed without the need to push your ISO up.

The low value of ISO is a great idea to use, but there will be a situation where higher ISO value will be essential to caption the best shot. For instance, if you do not have a tripod at hands and you wish to freeze motion, you could compensate for the fast shutter speed by keeping your aperture as high as your lens can go and compensate for the remaining exposure with ISO. The higher ISO value will help to capture sharp and bright photos.

Take control of the ISO and avoid the auto ISO mode

Using high ISO is only helpful when you don't have any choice to get brighten photographs in the dark environment.

You can use the base value of ISO in the dim light, but using 100 to 200 ISO in the dark will make your pictures appear dark. The same is the case with using too fast shutter speed to caption the action; the images will look the dark as well. So, in the darkness or sports, action using high ISO is sometimes the only option.

See what ISO you need:

- First of all, you need to select the desired value of the aperture to get the anticipated depth of field.
- Choose the base value of ISO and set your shutter speed at the value, which gives the suitable exposure.
- If the focused subject appears blurry, you can slightly raise the ISO and use fast shutter speed to avoid the motion blur.

In modern DSRL cameras, shooting around ISO 400-600 still delivers very good images, and it is usually accepted as the typical ISO for the majority of situations. Other times you have to boost the ISO, perhaps you wish to freeze motion, or you're shooting in the pitch black and want sharp stars. Precisely what ISO you need depends on the general brightness of your scene.

ISO for Landscapes, Architectural and Studio Photography

Choosing the right camera setting is always challenging, even for advanced photographers. Adjusting ISO for landscape varies with the timings and light. ISO controls the sensitivity to light of your camera. With the higher light, the sensitivity to light also grows, and with lower light, the sensitivity to light also diminishes. This rule is for beginners to learn ISO for different situations. However, the concept is not that easy to implement sometimes.

Landscapes are usually stationary objects, so using the low value of shutter speed is advisable. But being an artist, you should not stick to the same setting for always. The low ISO is also suitable for capturing slightly moving clouds over the mountains. It's also possible to use 100 ISO at night time. You cannot freeze flowing water at low ISO. The ISO has to increase with various situations while capturing the landscape.

Such as:
- To freeze the perfect motion of the water
- To freeze the moving branches
- To freeze moving objects in high wind
- When you are handholding the telephoto lens

Adjusting High ISO to Capture Landscape at Night

Using 100 ISO at night is not always a good option, as you might hear before as well. Because at night time, you need more exposure to light, and 100 ISO won't work out correctly. 100 ISO will keep the shot underexposed and very likely to be the darkest image. The higher ISO is used to brighten the pictures and to maintain the exposure of the shot. To catch the city light and moving vehicles, you can use 1600 ISO value. But to capture stars at hillside would require the higher ISO like 4000 to get the exposure to the fullest and to get the clarity of the image.

ISO for Architectural Photography

It is usually advised to keep the ISO low for the stationary objects. The experts recommend using manual mode, ISO 100, Aperture f/8 to f/14, and the shutter speed 1/125th of a second. You can change the ISO value to capture the building at night and midday light. You can experiment with different ISO values to get some different results.

ISO for Studio Photography

Studio photography can do well in the market by using the same conventional techniques to shoot studio photographs. Studio photography is also evolving with time being along with the evolution of cameras, lenses, and studio lighting. Studio Photography doesn't always mean using conventional techniques. It is a kind of expensive photography for it is used for commercial purposes, weddings, and fashion photography too.

Using 100 ISO is always a good start for any photography. You can begin with 100 ISO with 1/125 shutter speed. You can increase the ISO value for lower light shots. Because of studio photography, background, foreground, highlights, and shadows matter the most. You can use low ISO value with an aperture for the precise amount of light and power settings on the studio flash.

TIP: Although increasing your ISO might lead to introducing some noise in your photos, especially in entry-point DSRL cameras. However, it is not a reason to be afraid of it. Sometimes you are confronted with situations where you either increase your ISO or you end up with blurry, unusable photos. Therefore, do not be afraid of pushing the ISO up to your advantage. An ISO of 320-400 is well-taken by most of the cameras out there. If you need more ISO to make sure to expose the light side. This will keep the visible light noise less visible.

Chapter 5: Exposure

The exposure triangle is a common way of associating the essential three variables that determine the exposure of a photograph: aperture, shutter speed, and ISO. These three work in a triangle relationship and one must balance all three of these to achieve the desired result. Adjustment of one requires adjustments of at least one of the others. They do not only affect exposure but are also the largest determiners of the global appearance of an image. Hence, master the exposure triangle is absolutely crucial both for technique and composition.

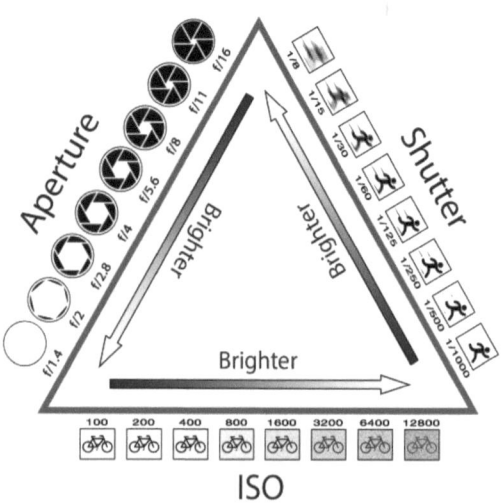

Exposure means the amount of light passes through the camera's sensor and how much is the sensor exposed to the light. To summarize:

- Aperture means how large would be the opening of the lens.
- Shutter Speed means how long the shutter will remain open and allow the light inside.
- ISO means the sensitivity of the light to the sensor.

TIP: mastering the exposure triangle is of great importance to grow as a photographer. When in doubt look at this triangle and think what direction to take. Maybe in the beginning, it feels overwhelming, but as you start using it, it will become as natural as riding a bike.

Explaining Histograms

The histogram is the photo editor of your camera. It helps you review the overall exposure of your scene, if in live view, as well as how the pixels are exposed in your final image. It enables you to decide the tones, final appearance and whether your image is underexposed, correct exposure, or overexposed.

The dark tones or shadows are on the left side of your camera screen. The right side shows the light tones whereas the middle section is mid-tones. Tones at the extreme left are pure black, whereas tones at the extreme right are pure white. Generally, it is a good practice to stay away from pure black and pure white as they do not contain any pixel information and cannot be edited. The high of the various peaks represents the number of pixels in that particular tone. In other words, the higher the peak, the more intense is the area of interest.

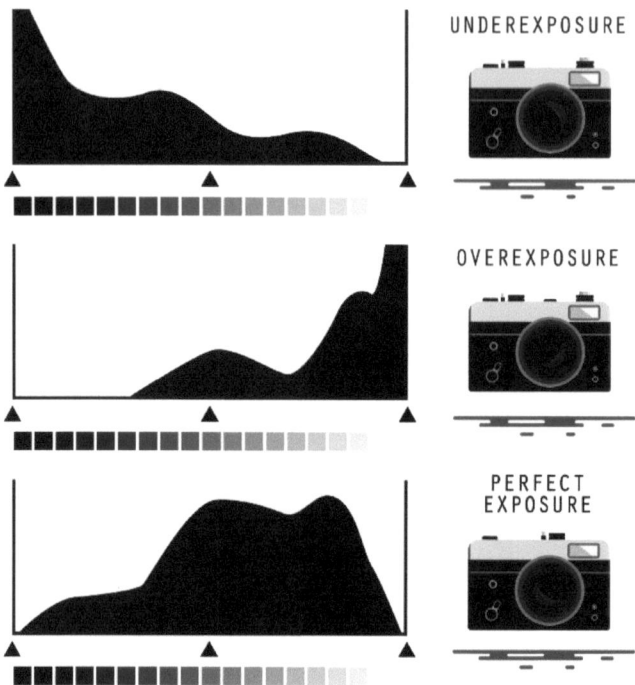

Now that you know how to adjust Aperture, Shutter Speed ad ISO, by looking at the share of your histogram, you can fine-tune the overall exposure of your image using the Exposure triangle. Below it is a cartoon that correlates the shape of the histogram with the overall exposure of the image.

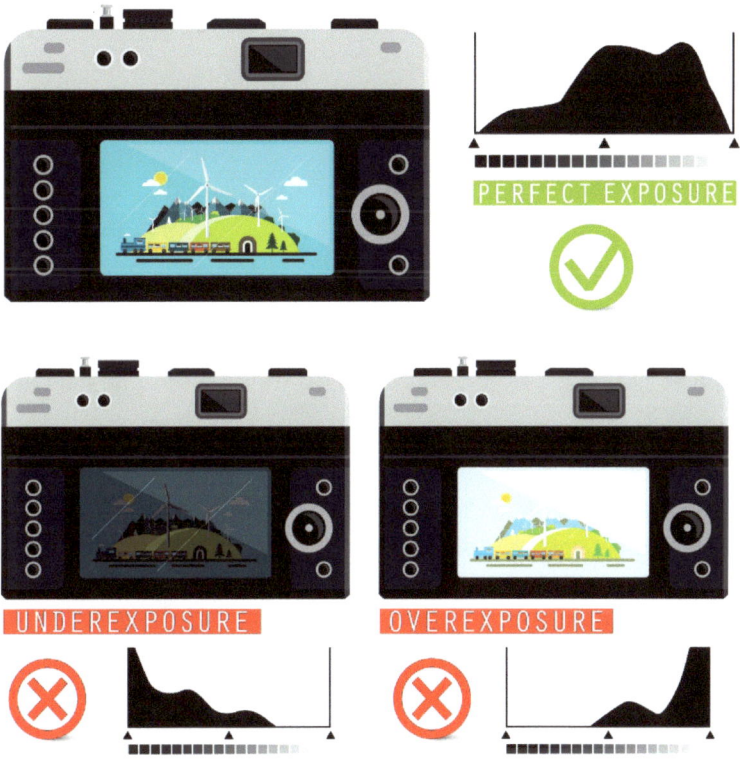

It is generally advised to exposure your photos such to have a nice broad histogram, especially at the beginning of your photography journey. However, there are situations where you might want to give a darker or lighter mood to your images. This means that instead of having the histogram somewhat centered, it might be skewed slightly to the left or to the right.

Chapter 5: What is Focus?

Focusing is a very important technique to understand in photography because without proper focusing, you will end up with blurry photos even when all your other camera settings are correct. When your photos are properly focused, they will look sharp and detailed.

Focusing typically takes place within your lens, through the glass elements moving forward and backward to change the optical path of light. Focus can be either automatic or manual. Automatic focus, or autofocus, is when the camera system drives a motor to move elements in your lens to change focus. On the contrary, to manual focus you need to turn a ring or a similar mechanism on the lens. Manual focus is used in very special occasions and I bet you will not need it that much, especially at the beginning. Most of photographers, including professional ones, use autofocus more often than manual focus. The main reasons are convenience, speed, accuracy and reliability.

In orde to understand what focus is, we need to introduce the concept of focal plane. In simple words, it is the distance between your camera lens and the perfect point of focus in an image. It can be thought as an imaginary line that runs across the photo, from left to right. Some people find it useful to think of the plane of focus like an imaginary window crossing the scene you want to photograph. Any object in your photo that touches this window is said to be "in focus." It is key to understand that the plane of focus comes hands in hands with depth of field.

Another way to visualize the plane of focus is by imaging to stretch a cord across the scene and ask some of your friends to stand along the cord. No matter how many friends are standing at the cord, they will all be in focus, even at wide aperture, e.g. f/2.8 or below. Now, if one of them steps in front of, or behind the cord, they will be out of focus because they stepped away from the "focal plane". Remember that the wider your aperture, the thinner is your cord. On the contrary, the higher you take your f-stops, the thicker your cord gets, meaning that no matter where your fiends stand, they will all be in focus.

Continuous vs Single-Servo Autofocus

In addition to the fully automated autofocus mode, modern cameras come with one or more additional focusing modes when using autofocus. The two most common options are:

- **Continuous-servo (AI Servo for Canon and AF-C for Nikon)**. It essentially means that your camera continuously adjusts focus whenever you hold down half way the shutter button. This is the focusing mode to choose to photograph a moving subject and/or when you wish to track its position as it moves. It is also recommended for most situations including wildlife, sport, action and for subject that involved motion. It is also the mode to use in a situation where your camera cannot be kept steady, e.g. due to strong wind, shooting from a moving car, etc.
- **Single-servo (One-Shot for Canon and AF-S for Nikon)**. In this case, once your camera acquires focus, it doesn't readjust until you let go the shutter button. This is ideal when your subject is completely still, and there is no need to keep adjusting the focus while shooting. This mode is recommended for steady shooting situations such as landscape, architectural, and product photography.

Autofocus Area Modes

A major part of focusing is choosing the right autofocus area mode. This is where you tell your camera what focusing method you want to use on your subject. Modern cameras come with several options when it comes to focusing. Although the fully automated mode is an easy way to shoot, remember that it is the camera deciding where to focus based on some algorithms, such as the 18% grey contrast. Therefore, the question is whether to let the camera guessing where you want it to focus, or whether you should take control and decide what it is important to you? The answer is easy; let's get out of the automatic mode and take full control! You can switch to any of the creative modes of your camera, such as aperture or shutter priority mode or even manual mode, and decide where you want to focus. Most modern cameras have a small joystick-like controller on the back that can be used to manually move the focus point(s) wherever you wish within the frame.

It is important to realize that the autofocus system of your camera is made up of focusing points, which correspond to regions that your camera can focus on. Typically, a greater number of focusing points results in a greater coverage of the scene. It also helps to track a moving subject when your camera has several focusing points covering a large portion of the image. However, you still need to tell your camera how to use those points. Let's walk through the most common metering modes modern cameras have to offer:

- **Zone metering (Matrix for Nikon or Evaluative for Canon).** Zone metering is the first mode to explain because it's the one your camera uses as default. Your light meter takes a reading from across the whole scene and it divides into many different zones. With that information, your camera's onboard computer determines the correct exposure with balanced highlights, mid-tones, and shadows. The number and type of zones depends on the type of camera you have. Nevertheless, most cameras give priority either at the center of your frame or at point(s) you manually focused on. For example, if you are taking the photo of a flower positioned at the center of the frame, with the sun shining on the back of the flower placed anywhere else around the center, your camera will take a dark shot because the sun is so bright than the overall average will based on how bright the sun is. However, if we manually focus on the flower, we tell the camera that our priority is on the flower and that the overall average has to be calculated based on the exposure of the flower within the scene. This metering mode is the most fully automated mode your camera has and it is meant to generally perform well in (almost) every situation.
- **Center weighted mode.** Imagine that you're now zooming into the frame slightly. Whereas the zone metering mode reads the light of the entire

scene, Center-Weighted Metering mode reads light towards the middle, covering between 60 % and 80 % of the frame. This has the same principle of the zone metering but with the exception that in the center weighted mode the camera gives always the most preference to average the exposure at the center of the photo. Despite the difference, zone and center weighted zone metering tend to give very similar results.

- **Spot metering.** This metering mode reads light from between 1-5 % of your scene. I personally use Spot Metering mode more than any other. It is the most precise metering mode as it uses just one spot to average the exposure by ignoring everything else in the entire scene. This is an excellent metering mode to use when you do close up work such as macro photography. It is very much used in portraits photography to get the correct skin tones of your subject. Another example when to use spot metering is when you have a subject with bright backlights. By spot metering, you can ignore the entire scene and exposure just onto your subject.

Some cameras also offer Partial Metering Mode. This mode reads lights from an area of the size of 6-15 % of the center of the frame.

Where to Focus

This is actually pretty simple; simply focus on your main subject. The sharpest objects in your photo will be the one standing stand out. If you are shooting a portrait, focus on one of the eyes. If the eyes aren't on the same plane of focus, then focus on the near eye. In wildlife photography you focus on the animal. However, sometimes, you'll have a bit of artistic freedom when you focus. Say that you're photographing a flower. Should you focus on the nearest petal, or on the colorful center? Neither option is wrong. It comes down to the effect you want to convey in an image. You can use this to your advantage. If you want, you can focus somewhere unexpected to draw attention to a specific part of your photo. Back to the portrait, you could focus on the subject hands rather than his/her eyes, even if their face is visible in your photo. There are no unbreakable rules for where you should focus. It's a creative and an artistic decision.

Where to focus in landscape photography?

What about landscape photography where you generally capture a wide scene rather than a solitary subject? Where do we focus to ensure that everything in the scene is sharp? The answer isn't always so clear and often it is driven by experience but here are some useful tips.

A common mistake I often see is to neglect the importance of both background and foreground in landscape photography. Many pictures are actually ruined because the foreground is out of focus. One of the simplest tricks for improving your landscape shots is to focus about one-third of the way up from the bottom of the frame. If you have something to focus on that is close to the camera, focus on it to make sure that foreground is in focus. This is how you can easily proceed:

- First, focus closer to the bottom of the frame to ensure the foreground is in focus
- Second, because depth of field extends further behind the focal point, focus at the one-third point ensures the midground and background is in focus.

Using the image below as an example, the one-third point would be approximately at the tip of the rock covered with yellow musk at the bottom. As a result of setting the focal point at that location, the rocks nearer the camera are in sharp focus, and the background elements are in sharp focused as well.

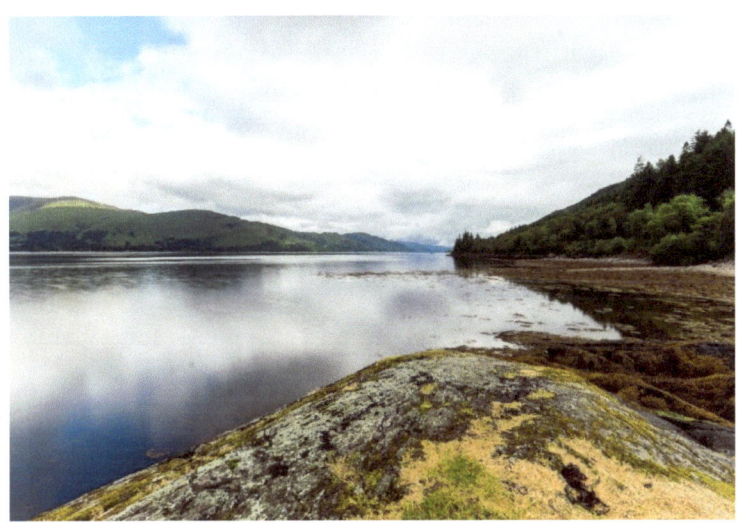

Photo by Fabrizio Micciche, aperture f/13, ISO 200, shutter speed 8 sec, focal length 12 mm

Obviously, this isn't an exact science, but with some practice, you can quickly learn to identify the one-third point and use as an effective focusing technique.

Talking about keeping everythings in focus, let's not forget the role of aperture and depth of field. This means that if you want a better chance of having everything in focus in your landscape photo, a smaller aperture is the way to go. However, a common mistake that many landscape photographers make, especially at the beginning, is to automatically go for the smallest aperture their lens can handle, commonly around f/22. The problem is that that no lens creates optimally sharp photos at its maximum aperture values. In other words, even though at f/22 you have a larger depth of field than at f/16, the results you get at f/22 won't be as sharp due to a phenomena called diffractions. So wht aperture to choose? All lenses have the so called "sweet spot," that is the aperture at which the lense produces the sharpest image. The actual sweet spot varies from lens to lens, but it is typically between f/8 and f/11. Therefore, shooting a scene like using an aperture of f/11 will give you back sharper results than iat f/22.

Having said that, remember that smaller aperture will cost you light. What is the consequence of less light reaching your sensor? Long shutter speeds (refer to the aperture triangle). Therefore, to avoid blurry shots, consider using a tripod or raise the ISO (risking, however, digital noise in your picture). So, just using the smallest aperture possible isn't always the answer. The ultimate solution is practice and experiment.

Recompose your shot

What if you do not have much time to select a specific focus point, e.g. a fast moving object? A solution is to use the center focus point and recompose the shot. Put your focus point on your subject and hold the shutter button half way to lock the focus. Then you recompose your shot by moving your camera, then you take the picture. By pressing the shutter button half way you lock the focus point onto your subject even when you recompose the frame. So why not using this technique all the time? There are situations where this technique won't work. A typical example if when you shoot wide open and your depth of field is low. Let's say you are taking a portrait and you wish to isolate your subject from the background. Your subject eyes need to be in focus whereas your background blurry. In this situation you work with a very thin depth of field and recompositing might lead your subject to be out of the focal plane. If you are having troubles locking a focus point due to poor contrast in your scene, try to use the center focus point as it is the most sensitive. Then recompose.

Chapter 6: From Automatic to Manual Mode

Manual mode means that you are in charge of customizing the aperture, the shutter speed, and the ISO to create the perfect exposure of your shot. The viewfinder will help you in the process so does the histogram. Although it might be quite intimidating at the beginning, the best way to go full-manual is practicing. Maybe the first shoots will be blurry, underexposed or way off what you expected. No panic! Go back to the exposure triangle and see what direction to take. Underexposed? Try to lower the f-values to allow more light in. Not there yet? Reduced the shutter speed to e.g. 1/100 sec. Still struggling? Bring the ISO up. As you get more acquainted with these three parameters, it will become easier and easier. Just dare to shoot and make mistakes.

Tips to get the best shots
If you have a camera, don't buy the new one

With the fast-evolving technology, new super-cool features, equipment, and lenses are hitting the market on a weekly bases. For practice, you don't have to buy a new camera. Learn the techniques and get the mastery over them.

Your skills will make you get the beautiful, iconic shots that will still look great among the pictures taken by the latest and best cameras.

Remember, photography is about mastery over photography skills, not about how expensive your camera is. Once you learn the skills, you can explore the market for the best equipment.

Mastery over composition

Composing the best photograph isn't easy. It depends on you to keep your composition clear, precise, and simple or complex. For beginners, keep practicing and keep it simple. To help you balancing your composition, use the rule of thirds.

Judge the focus, simplicity, and precision. Keep observing, keep analyzing, and keep taking shots. Remember to check your composition from different angles and point of view.

Observation of the surrounding and camera settings

The journey of photography begins from the shift from the automatic to manual settings of the camera. You need to develop the skills to adjust the camera setting according to the requirement of the scene your photographing. There is a lot more to learn and practice for the right camera settings.

Even advanced photographers don't do it perfectly always. Photography is an art that requires your observation, in-depth knowledge, and mastery over the camera that helps in generating the masterpiece. Focus on strengthen your knowledge on the exposure triangles, different auto-focus modes, and editing of the pictures.

Pay attention to the light

The essential source behind a great photo is the light. Taking shots in good light is an easy thing to get a good picture. But what about the sunsets, the sunrise or even moving vehicles at night? Usually, the main goal is to maintain the balance between the intensity of the light between the subject and the background.

Taking shots of the sunset can be ruined by a complete dark foreground. You need to have a keen observation of the softness of light. The harsh light means bad shadows across the subject.

Pay attention to where the light is coming from and position it correctly to avoid blow out highlights. Use the light as part of your composition.

Know when to use a tripod

One of the best inventions in the world of photography. It helps to deal with the trickiest problem of lack of light. It is best to capture multi-minute exposures and the mini details that are invisible to the human eye. For brighter views, a tripod helps to enhance the stability and sharpness of the caption.

Use a tripod for stationary objects such as landscape, still life, architectural photography and low light photography. For action, travel and event photography tripod will slow you down.

Know when to use speedlights

Although we did not cover the use of speedlight in this book, it is something to consider and surely practice when an extra light source is needed. Speedlights are useful for outdoors and to catch mid daylight.

Fill flash can be used to fill the bad shadows on the subject because it's a gentle lighting. Using speedlight in bright daylight can produce the best results instead of just using it in dark environments.

Avoiding using glares

Your photos will be facing glares when they are overexposed to intense light, and glares look as ugly as the shadows. Usually, glares are special techniques to get artistic effects in the image. But you need to avoid them if it underexposes your subject. Under the intense light, use the camera's preview mode and can check the required amount of glare through the viewfinder. You can also give artificial glare to your image by using photo editing software.

Tips to shoot buildings and architecture

Always try different techniques and approaches to capture the buildings. By using the unique effect of the light and the rule of the thirds to create some masterpieces. It would surely give a simplified yet beautiful caption to the building.

Try to capturing unique perspectives, for instance, taking a shot of the portion of the building or the structure. Try shooting architecture from different angles instead of just front and conventional ways of photographing buildings. Avoid taking obvious and boring shots of buildings. Take advantage of the surroundings to make the building stand out magnificently.

Tips for shoot nature

Capturing the aesthetic beauty of nature involves light, colors, settings, creativity, framing, and composing. Even ordinary camera settings can turn the scene into the serene beauty.

Profound observation and artistic vision can capture the contrasting colors. Using the rule of the thirds will keep the photo composition balanced and simple, while framing and lighting to capture the vivid colors of the shot taken from an unusual perspective.

Framing of the photos is an essential tool to create a sense of depth. The rule of the third will help you frame the captions for natural scenery. For example, to shoot the snow-covered road surrounded by trees is best to be shot by the rule of the thirds by keeping the snow-covered path in the center and the trees lanes on intersection points.

My final top 5 photography tips

1. **Take your time to understand and explore the Exposure Triangle**. Start with Aperture and Shutter Priority modes and use ISO to your advantage.
2. **Learn how to hold your camera**. This is a very important practical tip because the steady your camera is, the better photos you will take. Think about to flip your camera vertical sometimes.
3. **Change your perspective.** Dare to move away from the standing-still position. Change your elevation (e.g. get closer to the ground), your angle (e.g. try straight up or skewed from the side) and even your distance to the subject (e.g. get closer or go farther away). Combine these and be ready to be amazed.
4. **Take your camera with you**. Remember that better photography means shoot everything, shoot often and don't be afraid to experiment.
5. **Don't blame your gear.** Always keep in mind that your camera and your lens are just tools. No matter how advanced and expensive they are, improper and/or unskilled use will still deliver poor photographs. A skilled photographer can produce great photos no matter what camera they hold. Upgrading your gear will not upgrade your photography skills!

Concluding Thoughts

Learning the art of photography requires passion, dedication, and practice that can make your learning photography skills and photographic work stand out among the rest of the world. All you need to do is to keep taking shots at different settings.

Here begins your new journey to create something memorable and marvelous.

Fabrizio Miccichè

About the author

Fabrizio Micciche is a freelancer Italian landscape and portrait photographer living in The Netherlands. His journey into photography started in the year 2004 and since then it has been a growing and unstoppable passion in his life. He produces a wide variety of unique, custom-made and on-demand images including fine art and exclusive works. It did not take long for his talent to be internationally noticed for his style, composition and uniquely post-editing. Fabrizio features an outstanding list of achievements and exposition worldwide including finalist in some prestigious photography contests including the Siena International Photo Award, WORLD'S TOP 10 Landscape Photo Contest and Filmmakers shortlisted for Earth Photo. Fabrizio has also a passion for teaching and passing over to others his experience and knowledge.

Website: www.photoscapeart.com

www.ingramcontent.com/pod-product-compliance
Lightning Source LLC
Chambersburg PA
CBHW040325220526
45473CB00009B/2576